THINGS YOUR PASTOR WOULD LOVE TO SAY
(...BUT CAN'T!)

An Honest Look at Your Shepherd's Heart

Pastor Joel L. Rissinger

"I have much more to say to you, more than you can now bear."

(John 16:12, NIV)

ENDORSEMENTS

This is the book many pastors have been waiting for someone to write. Direct, clear, practical, humorous, and helpful. A great read for pastors and their church leaders. Thanks, Joel.

Dave Earley, D.Min.
Associate Professor of Pastoral Leadership and Evangelism, John W. Rawlings Graduate School of Divinity

One simple glance at the chapter names will give you a great glimpse into this new, profoundly honest, and transparent work by Pastor Joel. Ever really want to know what your pastor is feeling or thinking? Well, Joel takes us on an incredibly honest journey into the day-to-day life of a pastor and more. He navigates us through the highs and lows, as well as the minefields that all pastors go through, and then in proper fashion ends up offering solutions to the problems pastors face. So, whether you are a pastor or not, this is a MUST-read, perhaps Joel's best work yet, I give it my best rating!

Pastor Al Stewart, D.D.
Author, Teacher, and Church Planter

*Leadership can be lonely. Certainly, this is true of pastors. Their strength and guidance are imperative for all those who rely on them. But many don't realize that these leaders are people just like the rest of us. Pastors have doubts, fears, and daily challenges like everyone else. **Things Your Pastor Would LOVE to Say (…But Can't!),** is a riveting "behind the curtain" peek at the human side of those leaders that we hold in such high esteem. A must-read!*

John "Cadillac" Saville
President, John Saville Entertainment, Health and Wellness Coach, and well-known Radio Personality

Pastors and churches are under a relentless spiritual attack and much of this comes from well-intentioned people in the church who lack an understanding of the challenges of pastoral ministry. Pastor Joel writes from the trenches as a veteran pastor who has weathered the storms. With insight, wisdom, and humor, he gives a fresh look at the challenges for the pastor and his family. You'll have a renewed perspective of how to encourage and support your pastor.

Dr. Dave Beckwith
Senior Pastor Emeritus and author of *God Meetings*

The health and well-being of our pastors is an important topic which is rarely spoken about. We automatically presume that their lives are happy, grounded, and problem-free, but our shepherds have mental, physical, emotional, financial, and spiritual needs, just like the rest of us. Pastor Joel's book tackles this subject in a straightforward manner, helping us to understand the pastoral life on a much deeper level. And he provides a clear outline of how we can assist pastors so they can successfully continue their calling over the long haul.

Stefan Rybak
Broadcaster, Media Expert, Marketing Consultant, and Author of *The Shadow on My Heart*

As a Lead Pastor for 36 years and now a shepherd of shepherds, I can relate to the realities of pastoral struggles. But this book is not for pastors but for laity and lay leaders. Imagine the impact on pastors, their families, and our churches if we took the truths presented in each chapter of this book to heart. It could reshape our hearts, attitudes, and behaviors towards pastors. Joel writes in a clear and understanding way from the perspective of one with vast personal experiences of the reality of pastoral ministry.

Gary Weaber
Northeast Regional Director and Field Shepherd with Standing Stone Ministries

Things Your Pastor Would LOVE to Say (...But Can't!)

An Honest Look at Your Shepherd's Heart

Author: Joel L. Rissinger
Editor: Lyda Rose Haerle
Cover and Interior Layout: Michael Nicloy, Griffin Mill

ISBN: 978-1-957351-12-4

PUBLISHED BY NICO 11 PUBLISHING & DESIGN,
MUKWONAGO, WISCONSIN
MICHAEL NICLOY, PUBLISHER
www.nico11publishing.com

Quantity and wholesale order requests can be emailed to:
mike@nico11publishing.com
or can be made by phone: 217.779.9677

Be well read.

Printed in The United States of America

To my wife Karen—you are a blessing from God, and a perfect partner in ministry to God's people and our fellow shepherds and their families.

To my son David—my firstborn, intelligent beyond your years. Thank you for your love and constant challenge to keep me honest and on track.

To my daughter Shelly—my baby girl, who's not a baby anymore, but has two of her own. You're a great daughter, wife, and mommy. Your love of Jesus and willingness to risk all to share Him makes me prouder than you'll ever know.

To Alex, my son-in-law—you've provided the greatest gift a dad could ever desire: someone who really loves, cares for, and values his baby girl. I'm proud to call you son.

To Aadi and Bryn—my precious granddaughters. Love you!

To so many fellow pastors and leaders who have encouraged me and given me support for this work...thank you so much!
I'm blessed to have friends like you!

TABLE of CONTENTS

INTRODUCTION

I've been threatening to write this book for years. I've often joked that I would wait until I retired so that I could be completely honest and not care about the backlash. While I've said this "tongue-in-cheek," I do realize that some of what this book contains might be offensive. For that, I apologize—but I can't apologize for exposing the truth these pages contain.

Unfortunately, pastors are a dying breed. Research indicates that many of those who start their full-time ministry right out of college or seminary will no longer be in vocational ministry by the time they reach retirement age, 75% regularly think of quitting, and over 2,000 per month actually DO leave the ministry. [1]

I remember reading that we close something like 3-4,000 more churches than we start in America each year. More than 70% of pastors admit they don't have any close friends with whom they can share their struggles. Christian denominations, Catholic and Protestant, are finding it harder to recruit seminary students who plan to make a career out of serving our Lord Jesus Christ. And for pastors who marry, pastoral ministry ranks in the top ten careers most likely to lead to divorce. This is, in part, due to the fact that churches are often lousy employers. Churches normally pay less, give fewer benefits, require more education, and expect more time and energy than most companies or non-profits.

The sad statistics are plentiful. But why? What is it that leads to so much burn-out, moral failure, discouragement, depression, and just plain malaise among ministry leaders? If we say it's the expectation or demands churches place on them, why doesn't this change? Why do these factors seem to be worse each year, not better?

At the risk of over-simplification, I would suggest a single-word answer: **SILENCE**.

They say, "silence is golden," but when it comes to the internal struggles of most pastors, missionaries, and ministry leaders, is that true? I would suggest not. Swallowing the hurt, guilt, anger, frustration, confusion, and pain normally leads to even bigger problems. Thus, this book is an attempt to "out" those issues such that pastors can be more transparent and churchgoers can be more empathetic. My prayer is that this may help turn the tide and keep more shepherds in the field.

To that end,

Pastor Joel

CHAPTER ONE

WHY HE LACKS TRANSPARENCY

◆

**Pastor: "I can't tell you what
I'm really struggling with!"**

I hate plastic wrap. First, it always seems to stick
and bunch up after I tear it off the roll. Then, while
I'm trying to straighten it, it inevitably gets stuck
to something other than what I'm trying to cover.
Finally, even after I've wrapped the bowl or dish full
of leftovers, it feels like it's not enough. I mean, there's
my food…just sitting there naked. Even though logic
dictates that it's safe, it feels like I'm leaving food just
sitting out, unprotected!

But plastic wrap, like emotional transparency,
has a purpose. It's good to see the food to know it's
still fresh without unwrapping it. It's good to know

what's in the bowl without having to pry off a lid. It's inexpensive and effective to use cellophane to cover what we're preserving.

And, just like plastic wrap, when we are transparent, people know what we're all about. It may be sticky, but it's worth it. When we open up, people can trust us more readily. They know it's safe to share with and spend time with us because our hearts are open and not secretive.

But pastors often fear this. Why?

To be fair, they've been taught that they are supposed to "have it all together." But being human, they don't. Transparency reveals this and can lead to them being judged as unqualified. Literally, they could be discredited, defrocked, or fired, depending on the circumstances. And the flaws in their families are often attacked and magnified with similar results. Pastors have often learned the hard way, unfortunately, that transparency can be unwise.

On the other hand, sometimes the problem is ego. Pastors sometimes feel that they shouldn't have to be transparent. After all, they are "in charge." So, why should they have to share their faults or fears with the church? In his book, *Dangerous Calling*, Paul David Tripp suggests that seminary education has often led to pastors embracing the idea that knowledge equals maturity. Thus, since the pastor knows more about the Bible, he is more mature. Thus, he shouldn't have to be subject to scrutiny. This produces a lack of transparency, as well as many other problems.

I learned that emotional transparency can be good—like plastic wrap—several years ago. Just a few short years into my vocational ministry career, I went through a serious bout of depression. The depression was the result of severe stress. The denomination I was a part of had undergone a major doctrinal upheaval. In fact, every major doctrine had to be renounced so that orthodox, biblical teaching could be embraced. It was miraculous. Still, it was hard. I found myself standing in front of my congregation, week after week, saying, "Hey all, you know those things you believed for decades? You know, the teachings some of you lost jobs and relationships over? Well, just kidding—they were all false. Let me show you why...."

Some loved those changes. Others hated them... and they hated me for sharing them. The result, as my doctor would later explain, was a serotonin drain that left me in a dark, seemingly bottomless hole, feeling like I'd never climb out and see daylight again.

By God's grace, and with the help of my wife, a solid Christian counselor, and a Christian psychiatrist who prescribed the right medication for the right amount of time, I did recover fully. Most never knew. I kept it from my congregation and many friends as well...until God challenged me to become transparent.

Seven years after all this happened, I felt the Holy Spirit nudge me to share the story of what I'd been through. "No!" I responded, "I'll get fired. They'll think I'm crazy. I'm the pastor—I'm not supposed to get depressed! C'mon God—you can't seriously be asking me to share THIS!"

But He was serious. I wriggled like a worm on a hook, but He kept nudging me. Finally, I gave in. "OK, God," I protested. "I'll share. But when I'm standing on the turnpike with a sign reading, WILL PREACH FOR FOOD, just remember, this was YOUR idea!"

I gave the sermon. I shared the story. At the end I made a feeble appeal that if anyone there was struggling with depression, discouragement, etc., they could come to the altar for prayer. And that's when all heaven broke loose. People started coming...more and more and more of them. In droves, they moved to the altar, then the stage, then the aisles—all three aisles—almost the entire length of the church building. People were on their knees. Some were weeping. Most were praying, some for one another, some for themselves. It was so crowded on the platform, I was literally stuck, I had nowhere to go. I remember the piano playing as we prayed. I remember looking up and saying, "I'm so sorry, Lord. Please forgive my pride and silly fear. Thank you for this moment."

I never forgot it. We started several support groups out of that altar call. Wonderful ministry was born that day, but perhaps more importantly, I became wrapped in plastic wrap. I've decided never to turn back, but to live transparently ever since.

To move forward, the Body of Christ must help promote transparency in its leaders. This means churches being less judgmental and, frankly, cruel. It also means pastors being less prideful and full of fear. In a way, that's the genesis of this book. I'm telling you things that I, and many other pastors I know, might not have felt comfortable telling you. I'm being honest for the lot of us. I'm attempting transparency with the hope of change. I'm hoping church can be a place of blessing…even for its leaders. In many respects, this starts and continues with transparency.

It should be noted that transparency can be painful. Some of what I'll disclose in this book will hurt. It comes from over 30 years of personal experience and countless conversations with pastors in private where honesty was the only policy. The truth DOES often hurt. Still, just as with a surgeon's knife, it can bring healing too. With that in mind, wrap up in plastic wrap and dive in.

CHAPTER TWO

HE SEES YOUR FAILURES AS HIS OWN!

———————◆———————

Pastor: "When you fail, I fail!"

One of Satan's greatest lies is that sin isn't really sin, "if it doesn't hurt anybody." Truth be told, sin ALWAYS hurts somebody…in fact, it hurts everybody. And believe it or not, one of the most wounded individuals in the domino effect of sin, is your pastor.

Think about it. Your pastor spends his life telling people how to be free in Christ. He believes in forgiveness and salvation through the gospel. He also believes in the process of change and obedience as people learn to walk by the spirit instead of the flesh (Galatians 5:16). Virtually everything he does is to help people walk away from sin and, instead, serve Christ. So, when people choose sin instead, it hurts.

Now I know you're thinking, *But it's not his fault. I'm the one who chose to err. I'm the sheep that went astray.* This is true, and your pastor knows it. Still, when a sheep gets eaten by wolves or runs off and breaks a leg, the shepherd feels responsible at some level AND NOTHING CAN OR WILL EVER CHANGE THAT!

That's right. No amount of logic, no argument, no extensive therapy program—nothing will ever change the reality that your pastor will see your failures and the pain that follows as partly his responsibility. He'll wonder if just one more sermon, one more bible study, a better approach in your last counseling or coaching session, or some other option might have led you to avoid the problem you're having. He'll beat himself up for not calling one more time or for not visiting you instead of doing something else last Wednesday, etc.

Several years ago, we experienced a murder and suicide in our church. The murder victim had been a member since we planted the church about 10 years earlier. She was well loved and had served in multiple ministries in our body. Her husband suffered from PTSD and abused alcohol regularly. He didn't attend with her but did come to some of our outreach events, men's breakfasts, etc.

As her husband's behavior became potentially more violent, I encouraged her to move out and to take her young teenage son with her. At first, she did that, but after receiving some questionable advice from a lawyer, she left her son with his grandparents and moved back into the home. One morning, her husband shot her and then turned the gun on himself. He survived but eventually committed suicide in prison a few months later.

Now logically, I know that her death was not my fault. I know that the husband had often refused to take advantage of my counsel and help; and I realize that my advice was solid but not completely heeded regarding my suggestion to her that she move out of the home and file a restraining order for protection. Please don't write me letters about this, but I have struggled with guilt and sadness ever since that fateful day. I've played multiple "what if" games—What if I had reached out to him again? What if I'd been tougher on her about moving out and staying out? What if... what if...WHAT IF?!!!

I'm convinced that feeling responsible for the spiritual health of the sheep is part of a shepherd's life—and perhaps this must be so. It's a strong motivator and, to some degree, may be healthy. But taken to an extreme with no antidote, it can destroy a pastor—literally eat him up.

So, what's the solution?

I think the only solution is to do our best to "walk the walk" of faith. Notice Hebrews 13:17:

> *[17] Have confidence in your leaders and submit to their authority, because they keep watch over you as those who must give an account. Do this so that their work will be a joy, not a burden, for that would be of no benefit to you.*

There are several important truths in this passage. First, we're told to have confidence in our spiritual leaders. It makes sense that if they went to four years of college, plus another 2–3 years of seminary, and then accumulated years of experience in ministry, they should have some value to add to our lives. We're also told something no western Christian wants to hear—that we must submit (oh no, bad word) to their authority. Some translations even dare say "obey."

But why such demanding requirements in this verse? Some miss the ultimate point. True, an obedient flock—one that obeys the Word of God (not the personal whims of the leader per se)—tends to produce a more joyful, unburdened pastor. But a joyful pastor is not the ultimate goal. The author of Hebrews says that having a burdened, grieving pastor, "would be of no benefit to you." The flock suffers when the shepherd suffers.

I once pastored a church where one of the board members loved to brag about the number of pastors he had "gotten rid of." The trail of bodies in his wake was a badge of honor to him. Unfortunately, the church body itself was one of the cadavers, whether he understood it or not.

The often unspoken, misunderstood truth is that when we grow in maturity, the whole body is blessed (Ephesians 4:11-14). It's noteworthy that Paul starts this passage with a reminder of how pastors and other leaders have gifts and literally ARE gifts to enable this growth. If they are called and are working hard to fulfill that calling, nothing is more satisfying than seeing the maturing growth of the Body of Christ under their care.

And nothing will do more to prevent their discouragement either.

CHAPTER THREE

HE'S NOT GOD!

———————◆———————

***Pastor*: "Sometimes I feel like you expect
me to be perfect! News Flash—I'm not!!"**

First, let me be clear. I absolutely believe that
pastors have a responsibility to set an example.
Scripture is clear that those who teach the Word of God
are under greater scrutiny (See James 3:1). Having said
this, perfection is an unrealistic expectation. And while
most people would agree with this on the surface, a
closer look suggests that we actually insist that our
pastors possess what I call, "The Three O's." Let's
look at each one.

Omniscience

"What kind of church is this anyway? I was in
the hospital for three days, and the pastor didn't even
check on me!" I'd be very wealthy if I were paid

$5 for every time I heard this complaint over three decades of ministry. However, I'd be even wealthier if I were paid an added $5 for every time the person admitted that they didn't call anyone to let them know about their hospital stay. The expectation was that the pastor would "just know" about the need and fill it. Unfortunately, only God has this ability, and unless he spoke to the pastor about it, the pastor wouldn't be aware and thus, wouldn't respond. Sometimes, believe it or not, he just needs you to tell him what you're going through or what you're needing so he can try to help.

This expectation of "omniscience" also impacts other areas of life and ministry. People expect their pastor to be an expert on everything including biblical languages, marriage counseling, budgeting, leadership development, parenting, public speaking, and more. Nobody, except God Himself, can know all there is to know about all these things…and DO them well to boot! Instead, it's good for pastors to surround themselves with people who know and can do well the things that a pastor CAN'T know or do. This delegation helps the entire congregation IF that congregation will extend him the grace to take this approach.

Omnipresence

Pastors struggle even more with this expectation. Many churches expect the pastor, and his family, if not at least his wife, to be at every event, every Bible Study, every small group, and certainly every worship service conducted at the church. At the same time, he is to be visiting every sick person, spending 30 hours in his study to prepare good sermons, counseling every struggling believer, winning all the lost people to Christ within a 30-mile radius of the church, spending sufficient time with his wife and children, and much more.

Impossible!

I've often joked with pastor friends that it's too bad most churches don't pay by the hour. The impact on the budget for pastoral salaries would be astronomical!

Having a church board which will set realistic expectations for the pastor's schedule is critical. They must recognize that only God can be "everywhere present" and thus they can help the pastor (and his family) set and maintain proper boundaries based on scriptural priorities. I've seen some great examples of this over the years, where a weekly day off, a limit of two evenings a week for working hours, and other restrictions are spelled out.

Here's another factor to consider. If the Senior or Lead Pastor is expected to be at every event or meeting, this will not only test or stretch his limits, but it will automatically limit the church's growth. In other words, the church will never be able to offer events, meetings, services, Bible Studies, etc., if they conflict with other activities because even the most active pastor can't literally be in two places at the same time. If a church frees their pastor from this expectation, they also free THEMSELVES to be able to host more activities and ministries, thus blessing more people and giving more people a chance to lead or serve.

Omnipotence

I recently received an email from our corporate office at Standing Stone Ministry: (www.standingstoneministry.org). Standing Stone is a ministry providing support and encouragement to leaders. Normally, Field Shepherds like me, work to help pastors, missionaries, and others, avoid burn-out, discouragement, or worse. This particular email made me chuckle. After listing the basic details of how to reach the pastor who had inquired about us, the email simply said, "He's tired!"

I can relate. Many thousands of pastors labor for years without taking a regular day off. Some rarely take a vacation, and if they do, they end up combining it with a ministerial conference or some other activity which is, of course, work-related. While some do take sabbaticals from ministry, most do not. For example, I have worked for over 30 years in vocational ministry without ever taking a sabbatical leave.

But this is unwise.

The more fatigued a pastor gets, the more vulnerable he is to temptation. The more tired he feels, the more likely he is to cut corners in his relationship with God or his family. His messages will start to show it as he spends less time in the Word. He'll also become more short-tempered and less grace-filled in his approach to counseling, etc.

As much as it costs to give a pastor regular time-off, generous annual vacations, and a several-month sabbatical every 7-10 years, it's worth it. The sad tales of burn-out, moral failure, depression, divorce, and other epic devastations prove that our constant push toward pastoral omnipotence is a recipe for disaster.

Pastors sometimes have to be taught and held accountable to rest. Many are entrepreneurs by nature and tend to have workaholic tendencies. It is hard for them to turn off, shut down, and just relax. Having a friend or prayer partner who will remind them to do this weekly can be powerful. Reviewing the biblical principles of sabbath rest can be effective too. This all assumes that the church is sympathetic and supportive of this whole concept of rest.

Ultimately, we need to see the humanity of our pastors as a good thing. Jesus is the only god-man in history—equally human and divine in nature. Still, Christ's humanity is a blessing for us on multiple fronts. Notice,

> Hebrews 4:15 – *For we do not have a High Priest who cannot sympathize with our weaknesses, but was in all points tempted as we are, yet without sin.*

Jesus's humanity is a blessing because it's comforting to know that He can easily empathize with our weaknesses. He understands our pain. Isn't this also a good thing for pastors who are merely under-shepherds to Christ?

Of course, it is. The other factor here is that if we allow pastors to rest, they will be better at their job and that blesses us in the long run. Recently, my wife and I went through a change in ministry to focusing on supporting pastors and ministry leaders across the Christian spectrum versus pastoring a single local church. As we made the change, there was a period of "lull" while we pulled back on one to begin working on the other. I began to spend more time in prayer to prepare. I also had some much needed, while unplanned, rest.

The result? According to my patient, loving wife, I became easier to live with. I was calmer and more patient. I started laughing and having fun again. Whereas I often secretly dreaded social gatherings because it meant having to deal with more people and their problems, I now was looking forward to going out with friends and socializing. In brief, I was a better husband, father, grandfather, friend...and yes, a better pastor. Yours might be too, if given the chance....

CHAPTER FOUR

HIS WIFE ISN'T CHEAP LABOR!

------------------◆------------------

Pastor: "It's insulting when you expect my wife to act like a church employee for no pay or when you take her for granted as if she has to be present at every event, activity, service, etc."

Note: This chapter was written with input from my beautiful, smart, and capable wife Karen. After 30 years of ministering in my shadow, I'm thankful that we now serve as equal partners as part of Standing Stone Ministry. Her insight is powerful!

I remember having a long-term feud with members of my Finance Committee several years ago. The problem was that I knew we were drastically underpaying our office staff and wanted to fix it. I was just foolish enough to believe Paul when he wrote,

*For the Scripture says, "You
shall not muzzle an ox while
it treads out the grain," and,
"The laborer is worthy of his wages."*
(1 Timothy 5:18 NKJV)

When arguing their case to avoid raising wages, the committee leadership said, "Well, when Pastor Fred's wife was here, she worked 30 hours in the office for free, so I think we're doing pretty well now!" (True story—different name.)

When I was ordained, back when dinosaurs roamed the planet, the stereotypical pastor's wife was a woman walking 15 steps behind her husband, carrying kids, blankets, toys, and books into church. Of course, once she got them all situated, she took her place at the piano to play all the hymns for worship. She was expected to attend every meeting, every service, and every special event. She was to help in the office and serve the women's ministry, prayer groups, and perhaps Sunday School or Nursery as well. She kept a spotless house and, while never paid, also never complained—about anything!

My wife saw this and objected to my ordination

because she "didn't fit the mold." Karen is capable, smart, and very well educated. However, she doesn't play piano, makes almost twice as much income for our family as I do, and probably walks faster such that I'd never be able to stay 15 steps ahead! Having said all this, she HAS volunteered for almost every major ministry our churches have offered and has never taken a paycheck. She always felt that her generous salary as a school psychologist was enough and allowed her to be a tentmaker instead of being paid.

But should that be the expectation of churches? Was Paul's admonition regarding laborers only meant for pastors? Is it healthy for churches to see the pastor's wife as kind of a BOGO (Buy One, Get One) free offer?

No!

And apart from money, are the expectations placed on many pastor's wives helpful to the pastor or even to the church as a whole?

I read recently that pastoral ministry ranked in the top ten careers most likely to experience divorce. I think these expectations are part of the reason for this tragedy. I find it interesting that Paul's expectations for the wives of leaders is far less stringent and more about character than competency than our modern ideals (1 Tim. 3:11).

My wife is not only capable in terms of her career, but she has an undergraduate degree in Theology and has worked alongside me in ministry for over 30 years. I would think that might qualify her to sit with me on the board of many churches and to vote or share input. Yet, in many church settings, she's supposed to work in the office or work with kids for free, but NOT share leadership roles.

How silly!

I think most pastors would agree that the best way to treat their wives is as an individual human being with some valuable experience. We should let her and her husband determine where best to use her gifts. And, if she has certain talents and will work for 10 or more hours a week, she should be paid a fare wage based on the going rate for that job in the church's particular market or area. If she's interested and needed, hire her. But don't expect that she's a free bonus that comes with hiring the pastor.

We should recognize the unique gifts and calling

of each person. Some spouses prefer to work to make their families and homes the priority. This may mean they miss some meetings or gatherings to serve the children, etc. For others, they may have time to dedicate to these extra activities at church, and that's OK too. The key is to set our expectations based on the individuals involved, not on an odorous stereotype.

CHAPTER FIVE

HIS KIDS AREN'T PERFECT

◆

Pastor: "Your criticism of me, my wife, and our children hurts. Your expectations of my kids actually make them more likely to misbehave!!"

NOTE: I've asked my wife Karen to help me write this chapter as well. Not only is she an experienced pastoral mom and grandmother, but she is also a retired school psychologist with an impressive track record of helping kids with behavioral problems. I should also thank our 33-year-old daughter who contributed to this chapter as well.

Two stories come to mind when considering the topic of this chapter. One involves my daughter who became quite "clingy" after we left a church I had served in for seven years and I started pastoring another church in a very different denominational setting. One Sunday, a deaconess from the new church decided she needed to set my wife straight for allowing my daughter to hold on to her arm and play with her hair as they were talking. Apparently, she believed that it just "didn't look good" for our then 7–8-year-old to need Mommy that much.

My wife politely, yet firmly explained that she needed her mother right then and that it was OK. I learned of this encounter later and was convinced by my wife not to react with anger. What struck me was the complete lack of empathy for a child who had suddenly been removed from all of her church friends due to her daddy's job. Her insecurity was obviously caused by the fact that this was a completely new, strange, and probably legalistic environment where she was afraid to make new friends. PKs (Preacher's Kids) often feel this way because their new friends might be suddenly taken away as well. This is a common issue.

Another instance involved our son. When needed doctrinal and administrative changes were instituted at our church, one of the deacons became angry at me. In response, he started undermining my leadership and soon turned to one of any pastor's most vulnerable areas…family. One week, he told all of the Sunday

School teachers that my son had told him to "F-off" in the hallway. The obvious tone of this was to suggest that my son used foul language because I was a poor parent and thus biblically unqualified to lead (Titus 1:5-6).

Now my son is and was far from perfect, but he's always brutally honest. So, when I called him into my office to ask whether or not he had said this, he replied, "No...but that's a great idea!" I assured him that my question was NOT a suggestion and told him to make sure he acted with respect to any Deacon or leader in our church. I chuckled after he left the room because I knew David had sensed the problem with this man and was bristling at being falsely accused.

While not all attacks on pastor's children are this blatant, the unrealistic expectation and lack of understanding of their "fishbowl" existence is a virtually universal reality. It's as if we've taken the criteria from I Timothy 3 and Titus 1 to mean that a pastor's children should be able to part the Red Sea, walk on water, and turn water into grape juice (since some would say making wine is a sin). But what do these passages of scripture actually mean?

I believe the key is the word most often translated "managing" in 1 Timothy 3:4. Paul says that an elder or pastor must manage his household and children well.

What does that look like?

My suggestion to young parents, regarding this, is to reflect on whether they've ever worked in a company where everyone was perfect. In other words, did employees ever make mistakes or do things that were clearly wrong? Then, I'll ask them to share how good managers versus bad managers respond to those mistakes. They can usually come up with examples of both, "off the top of their heads." We've all seen this— the effectiveness of a manager isn't measured in how flawless his people are, but by how he or she responds to the imperfections!

Even God Himself wouldn't qualify to serve in some of our churches. Why? Look how messed up HIS kids often are. This started in the Garden of Eden, where Adam and Eve—children of the only perfect parent in history—sinned and destined all of humanity to be born in a sinful, godless, state! If perfect children are the requirement for pastoral leadership, God is no longer qualified. That's clearly a problem.

No, managing a household often centers around how we respond to mistakes, sins, shortcomings, etc. Thus, the REAL criteria is how a leader responds to the expected imperfections in his children. Does he overreact and become harsh and abusive? On the other hand, does he under-react and become permissive or absent? These responses might disqualify someone until corrected or changed. But HAVING imperfect children? That's to be expected.

I remember my daughter's rebellious teenage stage. It happened in the same church where my wife was criticized for letting her "cling too much." After a few years, and a dose of hormones via puberty, she changed. Oh boy, did she! Now, rather than cling, she was rebelling. Thankfully, most of it was harmless. Still, it became challenging at times.

I'll never forget the Sunday I finally decided to give a sermon on parenting principles from scripture. I had put this off for years because frankly, I was self-conscious about my own failures as a father. Still, I knew that the church needed a message on this topic, and I was their pastor—so I gave it.

The problem was that my daughter chose that particular Sunday to try out a new hairstyle and dress code. She donned an all-black, goth wardrobe, and dyed her hair what I called "Smurf Blue." It almost glowed in the dark it was so bright. She then chose to sit right in the center front of the sanctuary with her friends so that her hair would pretty much blind the entire congregation.

During my sermon, I remember feeling the pressure to respond to this obvious statement by my daughter. So, at one point, I said, "You know…as parents, we have to choose our battles. Some things, we choose to 'die on the hill' for. Other things…for a random example—hair color…we choose not to fight over or even note as an issue." The audience laughed and uttered several "oooohs," and my daughter jokingly shook her fist, but it all went over well.

Pastor's kids shouldn't be treated any differently than other children. All the same rules should apply as should the same level of grace. Still, it's helpful to consider their situation such that we can pray and empathize more effectively.

Picture yourself as a child. Now imagine living under the constant scrutiny of not only your family, your teachers at school, and your friends, but of sometimes hundreds of other people. Imagine being the illustration or example in many of your father's sermons. Imagine the sense of expectation that you have to be smarter, healthier, more obedient, more spiritual, and maybe even a better athlete than all of the other kids in your church. Put yourself in the place where your flaws are magnified and where your successes are "expected" instead of being celebrated. Imagine the feeling of having hundreds of eyes fixed on you wherever you go and whatever you do— especially at church.

How would that feel?

Now add to all that the feeling of seeing your parents suffer under the burden of leadership, especially when things go wrong at church. Imagine hearing your father relentlessly criticized or even falsely accused publicly or privately for just trying to do his job. Furthermore, imagine that you are not allowed to respond to any of this, but rather, to keep smiling and being polite to those who are sometimes ripping your parent's heart out, and watching you like a hawk looking for its next meal.

Now, can you begin to understand why "preacher's kids" can act out or be challenging to manage or work with in youth activities, etc.? It saddens me to see how many of these children grow up hating the church and walking away from faith altogether. I'm not suggesting that their parents have no fault in this, but I AM suggesting that their churches often share some of the blame!

What do your pastor's children need? Love, understanding, and people willing to treat them like everyone else's kids. That's it really. Nothing more… nothing less. Making this shift in our churches would no-doubt bless everyone involved and make the pastor's job a whole lot easier.

CHAPTER SIX

HE'S NOT WEALTHY!

———————◆———————

Pastor: "Why are professionals with less education and experience paid so much more than pastors? When I have to struggle to make ends meet, it distracts me from ministry!"

This is perhaps the most sensitive of all topics regarding pastoral ministry. On the one hand, ministry is service and is sacrificial. On the other hand, pastors need income to take care of themselves and their families. How do we find the balance in that?

Truth is, many churches do NOT find a balance. Sadly, the Christian Church is notoriously one of the worst employers on the planet. Beyond the common expectation that pastors' wives should work for free, the church often demands 60-80 hours per week at a rate of pay that equates to something far below minimum wage.

Now I know we're all sensitive to the opposite extreme. We've seen the televangelists making an appeal to fund a bigger personal jet. We've watched the exposés of megachurch preachers with lavish mansions, multiple sports cars, custom-made suits, and more. We've heard the proud claims of prosperity gospel preachers who see their opulence as a sign of God's favor—something they mistakenly offer to all who will "sow a seed of faith" by giving more money to them.

I wholeheartedly condemn these extremes! Still, the Bible is clear that a minister of the gospel should make his living from the gospel (I Cor. 9:14). It's also clear that the servant of God is worthy of a fair wage (1 Tim. 5:18). What is that fair wage?

I've always believed that the best way to determine fair pay for a pastor is to look at comparable pay scales for similar professions in your community. Look at the educational requirements, years of experience needed, and find a match. For senior pastors, their role may closely line up with that of a high school principal. Thus, looking at the pay range for a high school principal may help establish a fair wage for the senior or lead pastor of a mid-sized church in your area.

There is flexibility here and sometimes churches have to slowly work toward a more balanced wage due to financial limitations. Still, that fair wage should be the goal versus an attitude that expects the pastor to scrape along, barely surviving or living at the poverty level, thus causing hardship for his family.

This mindset should extend beyond salary to other benefits and expenses as well. If your church has a parsonage, is it well maintained? Would you live there? Is there mold or other problems that could be health hazards? If so, fix those immediately. Do you have funds built into the church budget that allow for him to attend conferences, buy needed books, etc.? If not, this should change as well.

I remember several years ago praying for extra funds to attend a conference on prayer. It was a three-day event with group sessions for all leaders in attendance plus break-out workshops on various topics relative to implementing prayer ministries in a local church.

As I recall, I needed about $800 for airfare, conference fees, hotel, etc. I was planning to share a car with another pastor and some meals were provided, so the overall cost was low. Still, I couldn't afford it, and we had nothing set aside in the church budget.

While praying about this one morning, one of our members called and said, "Hey Pastor, I picked up an extra job on the side and want to tithe on that project. I was going to just give it as an offering, but I thought I'd check to see if you had any specific need I could fund or support. It's about $800."

I about fell out of my chair. "Well, yes," I replied, "I was just praying for $800 for a conference I felt I should attend." I called our elders, and they all agreed that this would be acceptable, so this generous man's gift paid the way. Great, right?

Well...not so fast...

When I returned from the trip, a couple of leaders on our board were livid. They accused me of misappropriation of funds for taking this money and using it for what they felt was a pleasure trip. One of them interviewed our youth leaders and asked them if they would have preferred having that money for their program. He then made a case to our elders that I had taken money from the children to sit in a hot tub in Colorado (which I did do one evening at the hotel after the conference was over). The accusations and hostility over that money became so heated, one of our elders and a deacon almost came to blows.

Now I'd love to tell you that this was a rare, isolated instance in my church. Sadly, I've seen it repeated over and over in churches large and small. Many pastors are bi-vocational. Yet some are in that situation, not because of a lack of offerings at their church, but because of an unwillingness for their church to pay a fair wage.

Shame on us!

There is wisdom found in the Old Testament law, which Paul quotes in 1 Timothy 5:18 (NKJV),

> [18] *For the Scripture says, "You shall not muzzle an ox while it treads out the grain," and, "The laborer is worthy of his wages."*

It made sense to let the ox eat while pushing the giant lever running the grist mill and grinding the grain. Why? Because he was more likely to have the energy and, frankly, the motivation to keep going at a healthy pace if he wasn't hungry and weak!

I lived this out in one of my first jobs in high school. I was hired to work counter service at a local dairy bar a few days each week. The problem was that my boss was the stingiest human being I've ever met. He paid us far less than minimum wage because he argued that we'd receive tips. I ask you, when is the last time you tipped someone for serving you an ice cream cone? Right. Never. Then there was the grease in the deep fryer. He wouldn't let us change it until it was literally as black as 10W40 motor oil. Our french fries were so black and greasy, customers could wring them out! The boss even denied my cousin the use of our phone one day when his truck caught fire on the street in front of the restaurant. With flames shooting out from under the hood, he coldly said, "There's a payphone around the corner."

This greed created a VERY unproductive atmosphere. For one thing, nobody took initiative to do anything because of fear of being chastised. In addition, there was no incentive to try to move up or improve because there was zero promise of reward.

Now to their credit, many pastors serve, "as unto the Lord," and work hard despite their financial hardships. But how much more might they accomplish and how much healthier might our churches become if pastors were well cared for?

Again, I didn't say rich, I said, well cared for. The rule of thumb is a comparable wage for similar positions in their community plus benefits and opportunity for respite when needed. This pleases God and will ultimately bless the local church as well.

CHAPTER SEVEN

HE <u>WILL</u> CARRY
YOUR BURDENS!

◆

Pastor: **"As much as I know it's not
healthy, I often internalize the pain
and losses of the people I serve."**

One of the often overlooked, reasons for pastors
needing respite, isn't their heavy work schedule or the
intensity of labor they perform. It's not the hours they
put in or their lack of days off. No, the most taxing
element of their job is the pain they share with those
they counsel and support.

The frightening truth of this is that the wear and
tear brought on by hearing about people's problems,
illnesses, relationship failures, etc., is somewhat
cumulative and invisible. Many pastors function well
and seem to be fine, while the burdens they carry for

and with others are literally killing them slowly and softly.

I've often used the illustration of the Black Knight from the Monty Python movie, *In Search of the Holy Grail.* Even though they're missing an emotional arm or two, the pastor's automatic response is, "It's just a flesh wound!"

Truly it's not reasonable to have a pastor listen to someone describe being abused or beaten and not have it affect him. Holding the hand of someone who's dying, or crying with a parent who has lost a child, cannot help but impact that shepherd in profound ways.

As I write this, I'm just finishing a three-year stint as a hospice chaplain. During that time, I've prayed with and comforted dozens of patients and hundreds of family members who are dealing with death. When sitting with someone who takes their last breath, or praying with a family who had just watched their loved one leave the flesh and slip into eternity, your focus is on them, not yourself. It's common to be unaware of how profoundly death hits and hurts—at the level of the soul!

That deep hurt, sadness, and grief often "creeps

up on you" when you least expect it. I recall one patient who had been difficult, and her daughter had been virtually impossible to deal with. The patient was in a nursing home, and the daughter constantly complained about the staff at the facility and was even MORE negative toward our hospice team. Often those situations lead to a morbid relief when a patient passes because the torment and complaints are finally over.

Not in this case.

As I sat with this patient and watched her daughter loving her during her last moments, tears began to well up in my eyes. I held her hand on one side of the bed while her daughter spoke kindness and appreciation while holding her other hand on the opposite side. When the patient breathed her last, I wept.

I really wept. Not just a few tears, but a torrent. I remember thinking, *Why am I so sad?* I hadn't known them that long, and what I did know was that they had complained about all of us for months, despite our best efforts to help them.

Still, there I was—crying like a baby.

I thought about it later and realized that this moment was actually a release of months of suppressed grief. It wasn't just about this patient or her family—it was the combined loss of dozens for whom I had never grieved. By God's grace, I was emotionally catching up with the sense of loss I had buried.

Pastors, chaplains, and caregivers of all kinds need those times of release. Without them, there is a danger of health problems, anger, depression, or worse. This is another reason to promote days off, seasons of sabbatical, and more.

It's also a valuable thing to understand when seeking to know why a pastor may not be as quick to respond to requests as we might like. Just like Jesus took time to disappear into the mountains overnight, pastors sometimes "hide" to process some of what they've heard or experienced. They need time alone and time alone with God since some of this trauma can even impact their relationship with Him.

I remember standing in the hallway of the local hospital ICU with my son in one room to my left, and the man who had murdered his wife and then attempted suicide on my right (See the story in Chapter Two). My son had experienced a stroke at age 30. The murdered woman was a friend and co-laborer who had helped us plant and grow our church for over 10 years. As I stood there looking up, I remember praying silently, "What do I do now, Lord? What do I do now?"

Of course, I brushed it off and did my pastoral and parental thing. I prayed for everyone, did the funeral, spoke comfort to my son and to the murdered victim's family, etc. I really didn't understand the impact until a month or so later when reading through some contrasting statements about God in Dr. Neil Anderson's *The Steps to Freedom in Christ* booklet. About two sentences into the list, it hit me that I had subconsciously begun believing some of the negative statements about God through this ordeal. I had doubted his love, his care, his grace, and more. As I contrasted these things with truths from scripture, a wave of grief and healing swept over me. I was so thankful for the comfort that brought, and at the same time, I was frightened at what might have happened had I not dealt with this appropriately.

Pray for your pastor. Give him time to grieve. Understand that, while he wants to help you through whatever horrible situations you may face, he also needs to process these things. Once he does, he'll be better for it...and so will your church.

CHAPTER EIGHT

HE NEEDS ENCOURAGEMENT TOO

————————◆————————

Pastor: "I sometimes wonder, is there ANYTHING I do that makes people happy?"

One afternoon, I was working in my office when the phone rang. My head deacon called to resign.

"We've had enough," he said. "You're making too many changes, too fast. We just can't take it anymore."

Reeling from the suddenness of this, I sat the phone down only to have it ring again, almost immediately.

"Pastor?" the caller said, "This is Jeff (not his real name)."

"Hi Jeff," I replied.

"Pastor, I'm calling to let you know that my wife and I are leaving the church."

"You are?" I gasped, "But why?"

"Well," he replied, "you are just dragging your feet. There are so many things that need to change, and you seem to be moving WAY too slowly. We can't wait forever, so we're going to move on."

To his credit, the second caller was moved when I laughed and then explained what had just happened. Hearing that leaders were leaving because things were "moving too fast," was a shock to him. After listening to my frustration with the irony of the situation, he said, "Wow...you really are between a rock and a hard place pastor. I'm sorry. We're going to stick around and try to help you OK?"

And he and his wife did just that.

While a seasoned pastor knows he can't please everyone, it's still helpful to know that he sometimes pleases someone. Now if you ask him, he'll give you the righteous, biblical response about how he works for Jesus and gets his affirmation from God. And that's true. Still, I've noticed that God often prefers to provide this through human beings. In fact, He even created a spiritual gift for that purpose (See Romans 12:8).

I should quickly note that this encouragement must be sincere. Exaggerated, over-the-top praise is not helpful since often, those who speak this way are the first ones to attack if things don't work in their favor. I've often told young leaders, "Be careful of those who hug and praise you constantly. That hug could lead to a knife between the shoulder blades."

I know that sounds harsh, but I can't tell you how many times over the years I've been attacked by people who, just a few days earlier, had been shouting my name from the proverbial mountaintops. One minute, I can turn water into wine and part the Red Sea, and the next, I'm the spawn of Satan himself. It's the extreme insecurity of those folks that leads to both behaviors.

So, your pastor doesn't need false praise. Still, he DOES need sincere encouragement. I recommend a steady diet of this to balance the criticism that always comes with the job. He needs both—constructive criticism and encouragement for a job well done.

But don't we all need this treatment? I tell leaders all the time that we should try to give two to three compliments for every word of negative critique. Having been in leadership, managing others at various times, I've learned that I can ALWAYS find something positive to say about someone, no matter how difficult they are to deal with.

Years ago, I worked with an elder in our church named Carlton Green. Actually, I had known him before becoming his pastor. He had been the Food Service Director at the Bible college I attended in California. After moving to Connecticut to take that role at the University of Connecticut Health Center in Farmington, he started attending our church, and boy, was I glad.

You see, everyone loved Carlton. Why? Because Carlton loved everyone, himself. He was one of those people who would "light up the room" when he entered. Always smiling, he'd find ways to compliment everyone around him as soon as he saw them. He'd laugh and joke, but never with a mean or cutting remark. He was a joy!

My wife had worked with Carlton while we were students. She and her friend worked the line serving all the students and faculty as they came through for breakfast. One day, she and her friend showed up late. They jumped in and did their job, and Carlton complimented and encouraged them and others as was his custom. After their shift was over though, he called them into his office. They knew they were in trouble, but they didn't expect their correction to happen the way it did.

"Listen, ladies," Carlton began, "I don't think you realize what a blessing you are to this campus. Every morning, you're here—bright and cheerful. I know you even sing to people sometimes, and they love it! You help people start the day right, and God uses you to keep a positive focus so that we all do our best for Him. But, if you're not here or if you're late so that people come in and DON'T see you, it leaves a giant hole. They frown. They miss you. They ask if you're OK and when you're coming back. Girls, they need you here—I need you here—to make sure people are loved and served the way the Lord expects. Can you do me a favor and try never to be late again. It will mean a lot to me and to everyone else too!"

My wife and her buddy cried and apologized. Carlton hugged them and thanked them. He sent them on their way with more words of encouragement and appreciation...

And they were never late again!

I've often wondered how our churches would look if we used Carlton's approach with each other and especially to and through those in charge. I recently sat with a pastor whose church board used their time during his annual review to critique his sermons, his leadership, and his children's behavior. While he was working virtually for free, pretty-much seven days a week (they did give him housing but that was about it), they had nothing positive to say and left him feeling like a failure. Nobody is perfect, and he is no exception, but I know of several things he does well. The problem is that those weren't shared, and that hurt him.

In this context, I'd like to quote a pastor friend who used to say, "Encouragement…must be encouraging… to the person…being encouraged!" As obvious as it sounds, this is actually quite profound. I've known many Christians who tell me they have the gift of encouragement. Yet, they come out with some of the most offensive statements possible when speaking to others. They might THINK they are encouraging, but the listeners would likely disagree.

I think that to be truly encouraging, you must know a bit about the personality, love language, interests, and priorities of the person you're trying to help. For example, telling a pastor who makes his living by teaching that he's "not as boring as the last pastor," probably isn't very helpful. If your pastor tries a new hairstyle, raving about his old one may not lift his spirits that day.

There's also the issue of timing. I've mentioned that pastors DO need constructive criticism to make things better. Still, sharing your concerns right before he gets up on stage to preach is bad form. I once had a man tell me, right before services started, that he was leaving the church because he didn't like our worship or preaching. Talk about a "buzz kill"! I did my best to put on my "game face" and move forward, but it was brutal.

I'd also recommend that, when giving negative feedback, you also give some positive encouragement along with it. And do it with respect for the office and responsibility your pastor holds. Even the ineptest leaders in the world deserve the respect that their office deserves. I can think of very few people on the planet that I disagree with more than President Joseph Biden. Still, if he were to walk in the room, I'd stand at attention and address him respectfully as "Mr.

President." I respect the office even if I disagree with, and have issues with, the character of the man.

Doesn't someone who dedicates his life to the gospel of our Lord Jesus Christ deserve at least that?

Yes…and more….

CHAPTER NINE

LIKE IT OR NOT,
HE HAS AUTHORITY

Pastor: **"Sometimes, I wish you'd do what the Apostle Paul commanded. I wish you'd 'follow me as I follow Christ (1 Cor. *11:1).*'"**

In today's world, calling for us to "obey" a leader is a catalyst for war. Imagine the pushback were we to be in a room with the author of Hebrews who wrote,

> *Obey them that have the rule over you, and submit yourselves: for they watch for your souls, as they that must give account, that they may do it with joy, and not with grief: for that is unprofitable for you (Heb. 13:17, ASV).*

Now let's be honest with one another. Doesn't

this passage make you uncomfortable? In the western world, we believe in rugged individualism. We are free! We don't want anyone to tell us what to do—including pastors who are shepherds of our souls! I used to joke in one of my churches that the best way to get something good done would be to ask the church to do the opposite. Oppositional behavior is a social norm in many settings, including church.

But this is crazy, and it's crippling us. We have a net loss of thousands of churches every year over those we plant or start. We see thousands of pastors quitting to take secular jobs every year. We are watching statistics regarding divorce, drug and alcohol abuse, child abuse, depression, suicide, etc., IN THE CHURCH, becoming equal to or even higher than those statistics in the world around us. By rebelling against the ones telling us how to receive God's blessing, we're under a curse—and this can't go on.

I know of pastors who have been stripped of all authority in their churches. In some cases, they can't even vote on issues as a regular member. Some are even handed preaching lexicons and told what to say. I know of one church that forbade the pastor from suggesting that people teaching Sunday school or adult Bible studies should be believers. This idea was considered radical and divisive such that he was silenced and even threatened with possible termination.

Throughout Old Testament history, the people of Israel would often punish their prophets. If they didn't like what was said, even though the prophets spoke words from God, people would beat them, throw them in jail, toss them in wells, or worse. The result? Famine, death, disease, and ultimately, captivity.

Perhaps there's a lesson here.

In his book, *Bait of Satan,* John Bevere looks at this topic in some detail. He explains the biblical covering of protection under proper biblical authority. Conversely, he explains that when we step out from under that canopy, we're not safe. I've likened it to running through an open field during a lightning storm with a metal rod in your hand. You might not get struck, but your chances are much higher.

This is because Satan loves rebellion. It is what made him who he is. And since it gives him the opportunity to attack and destroy, it is his favorite "bait." Thousands of church splits, leadership failures, and perhaps millions of ruined lives have been the result.

Now I don't want to be accused of suggesting blind obedience or a support for any abuse of authority. The operative phrase in Paul's statement in 1 Cor. 11:1 is "as I follow Christ." Pastors don't have the authority to tell us who to marry or what kind of car to drive or what job to take, etc. I realize that there are many, many examples of pastoral misconduct and mistreatment. The disgusting sexual abuse of children by Catholic priests and the sexual and moral sins of pastors have left many people wounded.

But the answer isn't to take away all authority or to ignore it once given. I strongly recommend having accountability to a Board of Overseers or other pastors who will ensure that the authority a pastor wields is actually biblical, and appropriate. In my book, *The Crucified Church*, I publish a version of our church constitution, at that time, showing how this balance of authority can work while not taking away from a pastor's calling to be "teaching them to obey…" (Matthew 28:20 NIV)."

It's like a play in football. If the coach or the quarterback calls a play, and the offensive players think it's a stupid play, it is still better for them to follow his lead and try to execute that play as effectively as possible. [6]

Why?

Because if they do a flawless job with that play, and it doesn't work, the coach will likely see that the problem was the play, not the players. He can then change it or make note not to call it again under those circumstances. On the other hand, if the players slack-off and fail to do their part in executing that play, the coach may conclude that the play was good, but the players failed. Thus, he may call it again and again.

In church settings, following the lead or the senior pastor makes it easier for him to see which decisions worked and which did not, so that healthy change can be implemented. All too often, people complain or fail to give 100% effort to what the pastor is trying to accomplish. Many times, it's a passive-aggressive response which may blind him to his own leadership failures. Trying to follow his lead and make his "plays" work can result in positive fruit.

Let me put it this way: If your pastor is following Christ via scripture, why WOULDN'T you want to follow him? Furthermore, who better to lead? You? Your best friend? Some Hollywood superstar? Assuming your pastor is trained, experienced, and called to the job, he has authority and God says you'll be blessed for submitting to it.

CHAPTER TEN

<u>YOU</u> ARE YOUR OWN WORST ENEMY!

———————◆———————

Pastor: **"You keep making the same bad choices and then asking me to help you fix the mess that results."**

You've no doubt heard that the definition of insanity is doing the same things over and over, while expecting different results each time. By this definition, some of us are nuttier than a Snicker's bar.

What I mean is, we all are guilty of patterns of behavior that are consistently destructive. The problem for pastors is that they often see these and try to coach us to change them, only to see us repeat the behaviors and suffer the consequences.

This may not be the worst of it. In my experience, it is fairly common for people to blame God, and perhaps the pastor as well, for the pain they're in after doing something they were counseled NOT to do! It's like the definition I once heard for the Yiddish term, Chutzpah. A word meaning gall or impudence, Chutzpah, I was told, is a boy who kills both parents and then asks the Judge for mercy since he is now an orphan.

In other words, we sin, then we suffer consequences, only to then blame God for not protecting us from those consequences. If our pastor has taught us not to sin, he is accused of being insensitive or perhaps even the cause of our difficulty.

If he felt free to share openly, your pastor might tell you that this is very hard on him. First, he knows his counsel was ignored. Then, he hurts with you when you experience the inevitable results of your actions. He feels bad and, since he loves you, he wants the hurt to disappear. But then, when you turn on God or him, the pastor feels hopeless as he's now taking the blame for something he actually tried to help you avoid.

And we wonder why the majority of those who enter full time ministry in their 20's will no longer be in ministry when they reach retirement age.

While he'll likely never complain about it, I know your pastor would thrive in an environment where most of the sheep in his flock followed his lead to quiet waters and green pastures instead of trying to swim through tidal waves and eat rotten cabbage. I know we live in a culture that values individualism and rebellion against any kind of authority. Still, as we've already seen, obedience to spiritual leaders is for our own benefit not just theirs.

I once counseled a couple that was living together but not married. Knowing they were new Christians, I gave them a Bible Study on sex and marriage to read together. After a week or two, I met with them again to see if they had any questions about the verses I'd had them read.

"No questions pastor," they assured me.

"What did you learn from these scriptures?" I asked.

"We see that God wants people to wait on having sex until they're married," they replied confidently, "but that doesn't work for us. We're going to continue as we are."

I was impressed by their honesty but saddened by their blatant choice to ignore not just my advice, but the clear teaching of scripture. From experience, I knew that this could bring a curse on their relationship and eventual marriage if they didn't repent. I knew that spiritual damage would be done to their relationship with God, not to mention the possibility of unwanted pregnancy, emotional pain, and if they were unfaithful—perhaps sexually transmitted diseases, etc. I felt helpless, frustrated, and frankly embarrassed. Their families attended our church, so any stance I took regarding church discipline would have a ripple effect on them as well. They literally had put me in a "no-win" situation. This distracted me from other issues for days.

I've come to recognize that many of us live with a subconscious tendency toward oppositional behavior. If we're told to go left, we automatically choose to go right. If we advised to go up, we go down…etc. The confusing thing about this is that sometimes our opposition pays off. We do the opposite of what we are told, and we succeed. This reinforces our paradigm and makes it harder to change.

Leaders who work with oppositional folks often resort to reverse psychology to accomplish tasks. I remember a period of time in one of my churches where our team noted that whenever I preached about tithing or giving, offerings would immediately decline. There was a clear pattern of oppositional behavior where talking about why or how we should approach biblical giving and finances, resulted in the congregation being somewhat stingy. My reaction to this was to avoid the subject or find myself downplaying the idea of tithing.

I'm not suggesting that reverse psychology is good—especially if it means a pastor is compromising the truth. What I AM suggesting is that we all should pray for an awareness of oppositional behavior in ourselves such that we can use the power of the Holy Spirit to overcome it. Our choices in life should be made based on the Word of God and the guidance of the Holy Spirit in us and in others from whom we seek wise counsel. Of course, this includes our pastors.

We must remember that our sinful choices and repeated negative behaviors do not exist in a vacuum. They often hurt us and others around us and dramatically impact our spiritual leaders, over and over again. The solution to this is simple. Just stop. Get whatever help needed and move away from these patterns. It can be done…and has been done by millions of believers throughout history.

CHAPTER ELEVEN

HE <u>MUST</u> OBEY CHRIST

◆

Pastor: **"Even if everyone in the church feels differently, I have to obey Christ and His Word. Please try to understand that...."**

It's important for churches to see their pastor as more than a hired hand or spiritual contractor. He actually works for and is accountable to Jesus Christ. When I was younger, my mother used to tease that she wanted me to be a carpenter. We had a family member who had done well in that field. After I was ordained, I told her, "I'm not handy, Mom, and I'll never be a carpenter, but...I work for one (pointing upward)."

Pastors do get a paycheck (in some cases). They are accountable to the church board. They do have a job description they should strive to fulfill. Still, they are ultimately there to preach for and serve an audience of one. If "push comes to shove," the pastor must teach and preach what the Lord gives him from the scriptures under the direction of the Holy Spirit.

Sometimes, this isn't popular.

While the role of an Old Testament prophet differs, there is an element of that office that carries forward into New Testament culture. As Paul wrote to Timothy, a pastor must:

> *Preach the word! Be ready*
> *in season and out of season.*
> *Convince, rebuke, exhort, with all*
> *longsuffering and teaching. (2 Tim. 4:2*
> *NKJV)*

This passage of scripture also contains warnings about how people would seek teachers who would ONLY share what they wanted to hear. Notice:

> *³ For the time will come when they will*
> *not endure sound doctrine, but according*
> *to their own desires, because they*
> *have itching ears, they will heap up*
> *for themselves teachers; ⁴ and they will*
> *turn their ears away from the truth, and be*
> *turned aside to fables. (2 Tim. 4:3-4*
> *NKJV)*

This indicates that we should be willing to receive the Word of God from our pastors even if it's not woke, popular, or even pleasant at times. Are we willing to back up our leaders for preaching the truth, even if it hurts?

As I write this, I'm reminded of how often my wife has commented about the lack of popularity of scripture on social media. If you post a stupid cat picture or a pithy saying or poem, you'll get dozens of likes. On the other hand, post a powerful verse from the Word of God and you may get none at all. Pastors today serve in a cultural environment where the Bible is not popular. At best it is tolerated. At worst, it is rejected or considered destructive.

This is not only the case when it comes to preaching or teaching, the rejection of the Word—even in evangelical churches—is obvious in how we live, lead, and correct.

I was recently involved in a discussion with some church leaders regarding a case of church discipline. To summarize, it was about a man who, on a number of occasions, had written and spoken very divisive and hurtful things about pastors in his church. He had been spoken to and corrected and redirected at least two other times. I quoted Titus 3:10-11 which clearly states that the church should "have nothing to do with" such a person after one or two warnings. I suggested he be removed from fellowship until there was repentance and fruit. You would have thought I was recommending child sacrifices in the sanctuary! The concept was so foreign and repulsive to these folks, yet the scripture is crystal clear.

Polity is another issue where the use of scripture can get a pastor into "hot water," so to speak. The use of deacons, deaconesses, and elders who meet the criteria of Titus 1 and 1 Timothy 3 is looked at as "old school" if not problematic. Rather, churches often opt for "diversity" by choosing church board members based on a desire to "reflect" the congregation with folks of different race, sex, age, socio-economic status, etc. Some choose board members—especially finance teams—based on business acumen or wealth.

I remember reaching out to members of a large church in my denomination years ago. I was in charge of implementing church planting plans for our district and wanted to discuss these with these leaders since they were a church of some means and a solid reputation. Even though they had been in our network for several decades, the chairman of their board had no idea who I was or that they were even part of our fellowship of churches. He had no clue. No doubt, he was a successful businessman. Still, it was obvious that he had no idea about the spiritual realities of the Great Commission or even their part in our denominational structure.

Problems like this infest denominations in general, not just at the local church level. A quick review of many websites operated by evangelical denominations will show an emphasis on environmentalism, social justice, racial or gender diversity, etc. It sometimes takes some skilled navigating to find any mention of the gospel or even a standard statement of faith. But shouldn't these things be prominent and primary?

Don't get me wrong here—I'm all for the church reflecting the community in membership, leadership, etc. I remember leading an ordination counsel for the first black elder-pastor in a church I pastored many years ago. After the event, a few people approached me saying, "Wow, Pastor Joel! It's so great to see you pursuing diversity in leadership."

"Stop right there," I gently chided them. "PLEASE don't repeat that—especially to Jack (not his real name). I didn't promote his ordination because of his race. I promoted it because he meets the biblical criteria in the pastoral epistles. I don't ever want him to think he's just a 'token' African American on our team."

To me, the scripture was primary. Diversity, while healthy—and we had it at many levels in that church—wasn't the driving force behind our decisions.

The bottom line is that pastors or denominational leaders who put Jesus and his Word first, should be supported and encouraged, not attacked. If we do this, they will be healthier, and our churches will thrive!

Now, I should clarify that I don't support pastors using this as a crutch or excuse for bad preaching or poor behavior. I recognize that some use the Bible as a whip or a club to beat the congregation over the head Sunday after Sunday. Some pastors are just angry people who use God as an excuse to vent that anger to others. This is wrong and these people need psychological and spiritual help!

Having said that, a balanced Biblical diet from the pulpit will include teaching, encouragement, correction, inspiration, and yes, even rebuke at times.

Preaching the whole counsel of scripture will bring
that balance, and a pastor shouldn't be afraid to cover
all of it.

In that context, I should mention that preaching
about giving and tithing is perhaps the hardest because
it is often complained about the most. People get really
upset when asked to give. Studies tell us that most
evangelicals don't tithe. So, when a pastor explains
that tithing is a biblical minimum standard and that
it means 10% of one's gross income, people can get
downright angry!

Sure, there are extremes where every week, a
pastor is chiding the church to give more. I remember
one service I attended at a nationally prominent church
where three—count 'em—THREE offerings were
taken. There was the normal weekly offering, which
the pastor concluded wasn't enough. Thus, there was
a second weekly offering, and then, a third was taken
up to support a visiting missionary. I joked with the
friend attending with me that they might grab us by
the ankles, turn us upside down, and shake the loose
change from our pockets before allowing us to leave!

Still, tithing is a biblical principle. Thus, a pastor
should not shy away from teaching about it. I've told

pastors that when they do teach on this subject, they are helping others, not being in some way, self-serving.

A friend of mine was challenged by a mentor to think differently about sermons on tithing. He had stayed away from preaching about giving until his coach asked him about his own experience with tithing.

"Have you been blessed by tithing?" he asked.

"Well, yes—many times," he responded.

"Well then," his friend continued, "why would you deny your church these same blessings by not talking about it?!"

This resulted in a dramatic change in my friend's approach to teaching about money. It also resulted in improved finances in his church as well as in the lives of many church members.

The bottom line is that, if pastors follow Christ and His Word, they will be blessed. Furthermore, if we as congregants do the same, we will be blessed. If, like the Bereans, we search the scriptures and see that our pastors are teaching the truth, we can then follow them as they follow Christ (Acts 17:10-12; 1 Cor. 11:1).

This will mean healthier churches and happier leaders as well.

CHAPTER TWELVE

FOCUS ON THE MAIN THINGS

Pastor: **"Please don't become angry or try to remove me because we disagree on some minor point of doctrine."**

When it comes to doctrine, no two Christians agree on everything.

Take a minute to wrap your mind around that statement. I think you'll agree that it's true. A pastor I once knew used to say that the key to unity was to "Let the plain things be the main things and the main things be the plain things." In other words, he recommended that the things CLEARLY taught in scripture be the things we focus on. Furthermore, he would suggest that the things God would emphasize with repetition were also the things he made most plain and clear in His Word.

I agree.

Yet, I recently spoke with a pastor who was fired from his church because he quoted St. Augustine. The argument made by his church board was that Augustine was Catholic and thus disagreed with key items in their statement of faith. The pastor didn't disagree with the statement of faith, and the quote he used was true and in sync with that same list of beliefs. He was literally attacked based on what I'd call "guilt by association."

What a shame! I was almost disqualified for hire at a Baptist church because I answered a question honestly during the interview process, telling them I didn't think it was a sin to drink alcohol in moderation. I later joked that Jesus's first miracle was turning water into wine, and the first Baptist miracle was changing it back into grape juice. (Don't send me hate mail—it's a joke!) Even though this doctrine wasn't in their statement of faith, my different view almost cost me the job. We need to move past this.

Speaking of Augustine, he's often credited with saying that in essentials we find unity, in the peripherals we have flexibility and grace, and in all things, we should show charity. Sounds like a sound Christ-like, biblical plan. Still, we seem to have trouble following this plan.

Perhaps the problem lies in defining "essentials." I stopped doing ordination counsels some time ago because I found that when evaluating a candidate, every pastor in the room seemed to have a "pet doctrine" he wanted to use as a litmus test for this poor person. Instead of looking at I Timothy, Titus, and the 10 or 12 primary points of evangelical doctrine as the basis of our evaluation, we were allowing eschatology, millennialism, individual views of charismatic gifting, Calvinism, dispensationalism, and a whole slew of other issues dominate the conversation. Are we really that prideful such that we take debatable issues and use them to define our identity and our supposed "righteousness" as compared to others?

May the Lord help us—literally!

If your pastor preaches the Word of God and focuses on what is clear and repeated throughout, back him up! Sometimes, we can agree to disagree on the things that other solid Christians disagree about.

As a father, I knew that if I wanted my kids to understand me and thus follow my instructions, I needed to be clear, and I needed to repeat myself often. I couldn't just tell them on Monday that the curfew for Friday was "11:00-ish." First of all, they'd forget this by Friday if I never spoke of it again. Second, "ish" might mean an added hour or so. No, I needed to be clear that 11 meant 11:00, not 11:01, etc. I also needed to work that into conversations throughout the week. If I know this as a failed human being, how much more does our brilliant Heavenly Father know this such that he gives us clarity and repetitiveness on the issues He cares most about.

I would argue that this is the genesis of the primary points of evangelicalism that most denominations agree on. I've had people ask me about my denominational connection. I jokingly respond, "I'm a pseudo-charismatic, fundabaptipresbycostal with a catholic view of the church." When they look at me funny, I'll say, "I just love Jesus…the rest is window dressing." Most agree…that is until they're evaluating their pastor for his annual review. If we can change this, a lot more pastors might experience longevity in the pulpit, and churches might thrive.

CHAPTER THIRTEEN

THE GRASS ISN'T ALWAYS GREENER!

———————◆———————

Pastor: **"Comparing me to other pastors isn't helpful. I'm unique...so are you... and so is this church!"**

I once heard about a family traveling home from church one Sunday. Apparently, they were enjoying their favorite lunch, "Roast Preacher." Actually, the whole service was being dissected.

"I didn't like the worship today," said Mom.

"Yeah, and the preacher was boring—again," quipped Dad.

They continued complaining, including about how the pastor's wife was dressed and how the pastor didn't say hello when they entered the building but seemed distracted....

Finally, little Billy had his chance to contribute to the conversation. "I don't know Mom and Dad," he said, "I thought it was a pretty good show for a quarter."

I've often marveled at how people will complain about their church, and especially their pastor, while giving less each week than they'd pay to see a movie at the local theater or eat out at Applebee's.

Putting money aside, this kind of negativity usually leads to a dissatisfaction and a series of odious comparisons to other churches and other pastors. "Pastor Jones across town is SO much more interesting," they'll say; or "Pastor Smith is much more friendly."

What's interesting about this is that these statements come from people who belong to another church. And once they move to the new church, assuming they do, they rarely keep up these praises on social media, etc. I imagine they eventually find things they don't like about Smith and Jones too…and the beat goes on….

I don't know whether or not you've noticed this, but most of scandals in modern Christianity have been generated by pastors who were considered by most to be the best. Most were referred to as "the best preachers" or "the best leaders" or "the most successful church planters," etc. I could name names—but so could you, I'm sure. When their sexual, moral, financial, or other sinful failures became national news, how much did these "best" labels matter?

They didn't matter at all.

This is not to suggest that every famous pastor is corrupt. By no means. I remember meeting Max Lucado years ago. I was writing for a Christian magazine and had the opportunity to be part of a group interview with four or five other journalists at a Promise Keepers conference. When Max walked into the room, we were awestruck. Here was a man that had written more books than some of us have ever read. He was a great speaker, celebrated leader, and talented author. We couldn't believe we were getting the chance to meet him, let alone converse with him.

But before we could say a word, Max looked at us with a sad expression on his face and said, "Fellas, can you please pray for me?" There was a loud "thud" as all of our jaws hit the floor simultaneously. "I'm tired of my flesh getting in the way. I'm tired of having too much Max in my writing and teaching. I need more

Jesus and less Max! Can you please pray about that with me?"

With that, he sat down and bowed his head. Hesitantly, we got up, surrounded him with outstretched hands on his shoulders and back. We stumbled through a series of prayers requesting exactly what he had stated. It was an emotional, humbling, and yet powerful experience.

What I learned from this time with Pastor Lucado was the incredible value of humility. Over the years since that meeting, that's what I have remembered. It wasn't his great speaking or writing, it was, and still is, his humility.

I suppose the bigger picture here is how we choose churches. Most people choose their church like they choose a restaurant. If they like the ambiance, the food selections, and the waitstaff, they will likely become regulars at that dining establishment. If they like the building, the preaching, the music, and the friendly ushers, they will likely choose that church. What's sad is that scripture calls us to sacrificial service, not consumerism. Thus, if we feel called to serve in a local church, we should serve there whether or not the pastor is a Christian cultural icon.

Bottom line?

If your pastor loves Jesus, loves the Word, loves the people of God, and has a humble and obedient heart, praise the Lord!

Of course, you want him to have other competencies, but as we've noted elsewhere, the biblical qualifications Paul spoke of are character traits, not normally capabilities or talents (1 Timothy 3:1-7 and Titus 1:1-9). If these are traits possessed by your pastor, thank God for him, pray for him and his family, and encourage him whenever possible.

CHAPTER FOURTEEN

GETTING HELP

◆

Pastor: **"What can I do to get help when
I need to talk or just take a break?"**

Who can your pastor go to when he just needs to
talk? Can he share with his church board? Often, that's
not safe if he wants to remain employed. What about
his denominational leaders? Sometimes things can be
handled this way. Still, there's often a hesitancy since
those folks may have some say in his career path and
opportunities moving forward.

Some suggest that the best option is to have the
pastor join a pastor's prayer group. These can be
wonderful—a setting where five to ten leaders meet,
share, and pray for one another. I've been part of
several of these over the years and have found them to
be very helpful. Still, these fall short at times because

some of the deepest, darkest personal struggles a pastor faces, may make him feel weak, foolish, or just accelerate a feeling of failure when laid bare in front of his peers. As much as we hate to admit it, pastors' groups can become quite competitive as leaders begin comparing their attendance figures, budgets, ministry activities, staff sizes and more.

Enter Standing Stone Ministry and their awesome calling (www.standingstoneministry.org). Several months ago, I was surfing the web when I came across an ad for Standing Stone Ministry. I had never heard of them, and I'm not even sure why I clicked on it, but after two minutes on their website, I couldn't contain my excitement. Here was a ministry founded solely for the purpose of encouraging and strengthening pastors, ministry leaders, missionaries, and their spouses, etc. This was started by a businessman and his wife who had seen several churches suffer through moral failure on the part of their lead pastors. After much prayer, they determined they would do something about it.

At first, they bought property in Colorado and began bringing pastors and wives, one couple at a time, to rest and be rejuvenated. This caught on such that there are now over 15 locations in the United

States conducting these retreats. Couples spend a week being loved, prayed for, fed, and spiritually filled with amazing results.

But this wasn't enough.

It became evident that a week-long retreat option was great, but pastors needed more. Some pastors wouldn't or couldn't get away to one of these events. And frankly, some problems couldn't be resolved in just four or five days. So, to deal with this, Standing Stone started recruiting pastors to act as Field Shepherds to care for and come alongside pastors right where they lived and served. Field Shepherds, like myself, are often older, experienced pastors who have "been there, done that," with the scars to prove it. We can speak "pastor" and relate to these leaders to provide comfort and care. Sometimes, we just listen. Sometimes, we offer encouragement. Sometimes, we can get even more involved, helping pastoral couples with marriage conflicts, filling their pulpit for a season, or more.

In all cases, we don't charge for these services. While we're Christian, evangelical leaders, we're non-denominational and don't report to church boards or denominational leaders. We all raise our own financial support, like missionaries, so that what we do for churches and leaders can be given freely, without obligation. And sometimes, our efforts can make a big difference. To contact Standing Stone Ministry, please visit our website, www.standingstoneministry.org or call 970-264-9329. You can also write to us at:

Standing Stone Ministry
PO Box 11028
Newport Beach, CA 92658

Several years ago, a pastor friend of mine went through an ugly divorce. At his lowest point, he was living in a hotel, dejected, deflated, embarrassed, and hopeless. I called him one day and invited him to an informal retreat at a local Christian camp. Reluctantly, he agreed and spent the weekend with us talking, crying, and taking long walks with the Lord.

I knew this had been good for him, but it was much later that he confessed that on the day I had picked him up to drive to the camp, he had loaded a shotgun in his room and had been thinking of ending it all. Despite my ignorance of this, God intervened through us, and he's still serving today. In fact, he's happily remarried and has successfully pastored two churches since that time. He and I know the power of a friend and fellow shepherd.

But what can YOU do?

Todd Rettberg, a fellow Standing Stone Field Shepherd, had written a book called, *What Your Pastor Wishes You Knew.* His final chapter, "What Can I Do?" is classic! It gives powerful suggestions for church boards, individual Christians, etc.

Without duplicating Todd's great work here, let me make a few suggestions. First, go back through the earlier chapters in this book and ask yourself this question: "How can I be part of the solution for this problem if my pastor experiences it?" I imagine several ideas can flow from this.

Next, why not schedule a meeting with your pastor over coffee and ask the question, "What can I do to make your job and your life easier? How can I pray for you and what can I do to help?" Once you've used smelling salts to bring him back to consciousness, you'll probably have a productive conversation.

I'd also suggest you tell your pastor that you appreciate and need him. Encourage him...maybe with a poem like this one...

Joel Rissinger

Don't Quit!

When things go wrong, as they sometimes will,
When the road you're trudging seems all uphill,
When the funds are low and the debts are high,
And you want to smile, but you have to sigh,
When care is pressing you down a bit–
Rest if you must, but don't you quit.

Life is queer with its twists and turns,
As every one of us sometimes learns,
And many a fellow turns about
When he might have won had he stuck it out.
Don't give up though the pace seems slow–
You may succeed with another blow.
Often the goal is nearer than
It seems to a faint and faltering man;

Often the struggler has given up
When he might have captured the victor's cup;
And he learned too late when the night came down,
How close he was to the golden crown.

Success is failure turned inside out–
The silver tint in the clouds of doubt,
And you never can tell how close you are,
It might be near when it seems afar;
So stick to the fight when you're hardest hit–

It's when things seem worst that you must not quit.

Post-Covid, this has perhaps never been more relative as several thousand ministry leaders quit each year.

Another suggestion is to form a pastoral support team at your church. This can simply be a small group who will regularly pray for, send encouraging notes to, and help lift up your leader(s). This doesn't have to be labor-intensive...just an intentional group of people who love their pastor and want to make sure his job is not a burden.

I've been especially impressed with how this is done in many primarily African American churches. I'll admit, some of what is done is so far outside my cultural norm that it seems to be too much. Still, their hearts to show honor to the senior leaders is heartwarming. Often, there will be special parking and seating for the pastor and his "First Lady." People will bring them coffee or water so they can remain in the sanctuary as long as needed and desired. When introduced, people will respectfully nod and shake hands with a sense of respect and validation. Again, sometimes this seems "over the top," but my point is, pastors are less likely to feel undervalued or "kicked to the curb" in these environments.

Ultimately, we all need to pray for and respond to God's prompting for the health and well-being of our pastors. Spiritually, physically, emotionally, and mentally—we want them to feel whole and blessed. Thus, they'll be better equipped to help us feel the same.

25 UNBELIEVABLE THINGS SEARCH COMMITTEES SAID TO PASTORAL CANDIDATES

(From ChurchAnswers.com featuring Thom Rainer):

1. Our last pastor preached for 18 minutes. Can you keep it under 20 minutes?

2. The salary is low, but we will pay you a commission for each new tithing family that joins the church.

3. What is your political party affiliation?

4. What is the least amount we can pay you to come?

5. We do monthly cleaning inspections of the parsonage. You will need to make sure your wife keeps it clean.

6. Do you mind if we have a Christmas tree in the pulpit?

7. Your wife can't take a job outside the home because she will be too busy at the church.

8. Are you a Calvinist? (several times)

9. Will you preach out of the King James Version? (several times).

10. What do you think about coloreds in the church? (Sadly, several racist questions were asked, including one church that used extremely inappropriate racial language.)

11. Will you play at least two hymns a week? The old hymns?

12. Would you be okay if we parked another single wide by the existing one as a parsonage for your whole family?

13. Do you own a weapon?

14. We want you to preach for a month and see how it works out. (The candidate lived out of state.)

15. What is your position on interracial marriages?

16. If you came here, we would want you to fire the youth minister. Would you be willing to do that?

17. Do you let the singers hold the microphones themselves?

18. Have you ever held a rattlesnake?

19. Would you be willing to shave your facial hair?

20. You have to mow the parsonage lawn at the same time they mow the church yard.

21. The pastor's office hours are 9 to 5 Monday through Friday.

22. When discovering the pastoral candidate had a physical disability, the search committee person said, "Oh, we don't want a pastor that's disabled. You have to stand while you are preaching."

23. What are your views on mixed bathing?

24. Boxers or briefs?

25. How's your sex life?

CHUCK SWINDOLL'S ADVICE FOR LEADERS

Chuck Swindoll, accepting a Lifetime Achievement Award several years ago, offered the following lessons he has learned as a pastor and leader in the church over the past 50 years:

1. It's lonely to lead. Leadership involves tough decisions. The tougher the decision, the lonelier it is.

2. It's dangerous to succeed. I'm most concerned for those who aren't even 30 and are very gifted and successful. Sometimes God uses someone right out of youth, but usually he uses leaders who have been crushed.

3. It's hardest at home. No one ever told me this in Seminary.

4. It's essential to be real. If there's one realm where phoniness is common, it's among leaders. Stay real.

5. It's painful to obey. The Lord will direct you to do some things that won't be your choice. Invariably you will give up what you want to do for the cross.

6. Brokenness and failure are necessary.

7. Attitude is more important than actions. Your family may not have told you: some of you are hard to be around. A bad attitude overshadows good actions.

8. Integrity eclipses image. Today we highlight image. But it's what you're doing behind the scenes.

9. God's way is better than my way.

10. Christlikeness begins and ends with humility.

14 SURPRISING FACTS ABOUT PASTORS

By Josh Weidmann

From www.churchleaders.com

This article about facts about pastors
Originally appeared at www.joshweidmann.com

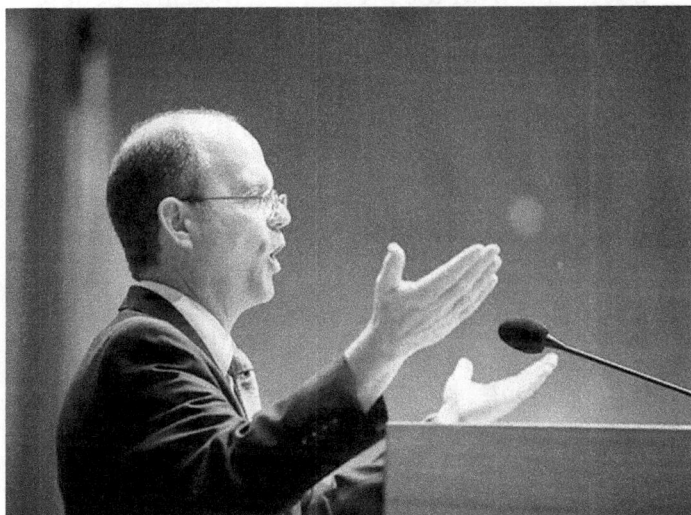

By definition, a **pastor** is one who "shepherds his flock." You know this means he preaches, officiates weddings, and probably has meetings in his office to explain some theological question; but what is the role of pastor really like? There are some common facts about pastors you might be unaware of.

Here are 14 surprising facts about pastors
that you might not know:

1. **We fight the balance between pleasing people
    and pleasing God every day**. We do what we
    do because we love God…and people. Trying
    to please both is a common reason for pastor-
    burnout, in part because people and God don't
    always want the same thing. Pleasing God wins,
    but living with the pressure of pleasing people
    can be extremely draining.

2. **We often hear more negative than positive
    feedback**. People assume pastors get praised
    often for their good sermons. Not true. One of
    the unfortunate facts about pastors is that we hear
    complaints often and more readily than we hear
    compliments. Healthy pastors can live without a
    lot of compliments (at least they should be able
    to), but the reality is we often hear much more
    negative than positive feedback on the preaching,
    worship service, theological points, etc.

3. **We say "no" because we love our sheep**. Pastors
    have families and lives too. We have to say "no"
    sometimes in order to be a good dad, a present
    husband, a good friend, or for self-care. When a

pastor says "no" to a church event, it should not be received as an indication that the pastor does not love the sheep but as a protective measure for the greater good of the church body so the pastor can continue serving them well.

4. **Our families feel the weight of our calling more than they will ever tell you**. My kids are young, yet they feel the weight I bring home at times. So does my wife. Pastor's families are well aware of what they do and **even the youngest member** will feel the weight of what it means to lead a church. Be mindful that pastors are not called to serve without it affecting the family who is called, even if by default, to be in the ministry alongside them.

5. **Eating well, exercising well, and sleeping well is hard work for us**. Pastors are often selfless to a fault. We will more quickly go serve someone than go to work out, sleep, or prioritize self-care. While it may sound nice for a pastor to be selfless and think of others first, there is a balance to be practiced, or it will not be good for the pastor or for the person being served.

6. **Many of us are "professional extroverts."**
Pastors have to do a lot of deep thinking and study.
We are used to being alone and actually love it
(most of us). We enjoy our time with people too,
but we are often professional extroverts, relating to
crowds and leading people out of a secondary set of
gifts.

7. **We know we could get paid better doing
something else, but we don't want to**. We can't
do anything else. We could…but we "can't"
because this is what we love the most and are
called to do. We stay even though we don't always
feel it. **Having a calling** is more than a feeling—
we grapple with that reality regularly.

8. **Spiritual warfare is a way of life**. The devil hates
all Christians. I used to say that there is no way he
"hates" or targets pastors more. But the longer that
I do this, the more I realize that the widespread
repercussions from a leader who falls puts an
automatic target on the pastor's back at which the
enemy can lob his arrows. **Spiritual warfare** is just
part of the occupational hazard for a pastor.

9. **We are always fighting our own sin too**. Pastors
are far from perfect. We have our own sins that we

are always fighting. Be patient with us. Pray for us.

10. **It takes us about seven days to "unplug" for a meaningful and true vacation**. It is REALLY hard for pastors to unplug. When we go on vacation, it can take up to a week for us to unwind before we are fully present. I try to take one two-week vacation a year just so that I can have one week where I am really unplugged.

11. **It is hard for us to have friends**. People assume we have lots of friends. Most of us don't. Think about it—our church is our place of worship, our place of work, and our friend circle; not three different contexts—all the same one. The leadership role of "pastor" is not a hat that can be easily set aside in those contexts. That makes it **difficult to have friends**. We also struggle with people who treat us as a friend and not a "pastor." It is not impossible for us to have friends, but it takes effort, and sometimes our best friends are not in the churches where we serve.

12. **We work more than one day a week**. People joke with me (almost weekly?) that I "only work one day a week, what is the big deal?" I know

they are joking, but it is obviously not true. Due to most modern pastors being expected to fill roles that are both spiritual and administrative, most of us only have one day OFF a week. It takes a lot of intentionality for us to have two days off a week. Pray for your pastor in this and, if you can, help him have times of rest. He needs them.

13. **Our greatest joy is when our sheep "get it."** When people understand what we are discipling them toward, or when a person "gets" salvation, we love it. That is why we do this. We want them to **love Christ** and we love it when they "get it."

14. **We are rewarded by being invited into a full spectrum of life's big moments**. Think about it, what other roles get to be an intimate part of births, deaths, baptisms, marriages, salvations, sacred holidays, struggles and victories? A physician tends to births and deaths. A counselor tends to struggles and victories. A pastor has the privilege of being invited into a full spectrum of the "moments" in lives of people he loves and serves. It is deeply rewarding and is one of the special gifts that makes it all worthwhile.

RECOMMENDED READING

Bevere, John, *Bait of Satan,* Charisma Media, 2004,
ISBN:159185413X

Rettberg, Todd, *What Your Pastor Wishes You Knew,*
New Harbor Press, 2021, ISBN 978-1-63357-405-2

Rainer, Thom S., Geiger, Eric, *Simple Church,* B&H
Publishing Group, 2006, ISBN 0805443908

Rissinger, Joel, *The Crucified Church*, Xulon
Publishing, 2010, ISBN 9781609578046.

Ramsey, Dave, *The Total Money Makeover,* Thomas
Nelson, First Edition, (September 1, 2003), ISBN-10:
0785263268

Tripp, Paul David, *Dangerous Calling,* Crossway,
2012, ISBN: 1433535823

Cymbala, Jim, Merrill, Dean, *Fresh Wind, Fresh Fire,*
Zondervan, 2003, ISBN 0310251532

Olson, David T., *The American Church in Crisis*,
Tynsdale, 2005, ISBN 13:978-0-310-27713-2

Hybels, Bill, Mittleberg, Mark, Strobel, Lee, *Becoming a Contagious Christian*, Zondervan, 2007, ISBN 0310257875

ABOUT THE AUTHOR

In addition to his role as Shepherd with Standing Stone Ministries, Pastor Joel L. Rissinger is the President of The Rissinger Resource Group, LLC, a certified speaker and coach with the John Maxwell Group, and a Founding Pastor of LifeWay Church in Newington, Connecticut.

More importantly, he has been married to Karen Rissinger for more than 37 years. Together, they have two adult children, an awesome son-in-law, and two beautiful granddaughters.

Since 1992, Pastor Joel has been in vocational ministry but has kept his hand in business as well. Joel has been ordained by Converge USA as well as two other organizations. In this capacity, he has led several congregations through major transitions prior to planting a church in 2007. In addition, Joel has served as the Director of Church Multiplication for Converge Northeast, the New England Regional Coordinator for The Antioch School of Leadership Development, Seminar Presenter for Life Innovations, Inc., and as a Chaplain for several local companies.

Pastor Joel has been a regular speaker at the Northeast Regional Iron Sharpens Iron Conferences, the Newington, Connecticut, Chamber of Commerce meetings, numerous Rotary Clubs, the Connecticut Better Business Bureau, and other venues. He has a BA in theology from Ambassador University, and MAs in both religion and religious education from Liberty University. He is the author of several books, including *Champion That Change, Communicate to Lead,* and *The Crucified Church.*

ENDNOTES

1 At any given time, 75% of pastors in America want to
  quit. (Church Resource Ministries – 1998)
    More than 2000 pastors are leaving the ministry
    each month. (Marble Retreat Center 2001)

2 1991 Survey of Pastors (Fuller Institute of Church
  Growth)

3 The 10 occupations with the highest divorce rates,
  Google search results, 5/5/22

4 Tripp, Paul David, *Dangerous Calling, 2012,
  Crossway* ISBN: 1433535823

5 Bevere, John, *Bait of Satan,* Charisma Media, 2004,
  ISBN:159185413X

6 Rissinger, Joel, *The Crucified Church*, Xulon
  Publishing, 2010, ISBN: 9781609578046.

7 Rettberg, Todd, *What Your Pastor Wishes You Knew,*
  New Harbor Press, 2021, ISBN: 978-1-63357-405-2

www.ingramcontent.com/pod-product-compliance
Lightning Source LLC
Chambersburg PA
CBHW060359090426
42734CB00011B/2186